WRITING RIGHT

KIDS BEST GUIDE TO LEARNING HOW TO READ AND WRITE

Sheldon Green

Dedication

To my five year old daughter and all the amazing kids out there.

ALPHABETS

A B C

D E F

G H I

ALPHABETS

J K L

M N O

P Q R

ALPHABETS

S T U

V W X

Y Z

Module 1

Learn

APPLE

ELEPHANT

TREE

Write

Module 1

Write

Module 1

Write

Module 1

Module 2

Learn

CAT

PARROT

HOUSE

Write

Module 2

Write

Module 2

Write

Module 2

Module 3

Learn

BOY

FISH

CAR

Write

Module 3

Write

Module 3

Write

Module 3

_____ _____ _____ ____

Module 4

Learn

BOOK

FOOTBALL

GIRL

Write

Module 4

Write

Module 4

____ ____ ____ ____

Write

Module 4

Module 5

Learn

ORANGE

BOX

BURGER

Write

Module 5

Write

Module 5

Write

Module 5

____ ____ ____ ___

PAINT THE ORANGE

PAINT THE FRUIT

PAINT THE FRUIT

COMPLETE THE DRAWING

Work 4

COMPLETE THE DRAWING

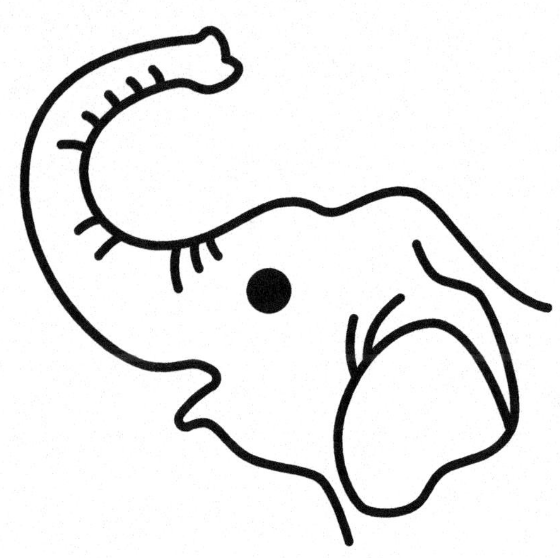

Practice here

Practice here

www.ingramcontent.com/pod-product-compliance
Lightning Source LLC
LaVergne TN
LVHW080559160826
845677LV00010B/1920
* 9 7 9 8 3 5 2 3 8 1 6 7 0 *